Also by James Blaine:

Pathways to a Closer Walk
**A study guide to the
Bible's relationship analogies**

*Some of James Blaine's other writing
can be found at:*
https://www.willhoft.net/jamesblaine

*Study Guides and Questions for Individuals and Groups
based on this book can be found at:*
https://www.willhoft.net/messiahstudy

The

ROLLOUT

of the

MESSIAH

from Eden to Ascension

James A. Blaine

WESTBOW
PRESS®
A DIVISION OF THOMAS NELSON
& ZONDERVAN

WestBow Press books may be ordered through booksellers or by contacting:

WestBow Press
A Division of Thomas Nelson & Zondervan
1663 Liberty Drive
Bloomington, IN 47403
www.westbowpress.com
844-714-3454

ISBN: 979-8-3850-0985-5 (sc)
ISBN: 979-8-3850-0986-2 (e)

Library of Congress Control Number: 2023919422

Print information available on the last page.

WestBow Press rev. date: 11/30/2023

Dedicated to:

The memory of **Dr. Wilber T. Dayton,**
Professor in Greek studies, advisor, helpful friend

The memory of **Rev. James E. Bence,**
Respected superintendent, wise counselor, kind friend

Rev. Wayne B. Wager, Sr.
Partner in ministry, faithful friend

CONTENTS

THE "ROLLOUT" OF THE MESSIAH

Rollout (def.):   the public introduction, or inauguration, of a product, a person, or of some policy.

INTRODUCTION

One of my first jobs was a most interesting one. In my senior year of high school (1947), I had only a couple of morning classes. Thus, I was able to be hired as a part-time office assistant (a "go-for") in the advertising department of Armour & Company, a major meat packing firm in Chicago's Union Stock Yards.

That department was composed of writers, artists, and graphic designers who, among their work, composed the wording, layouts, and designs of full-page ads to be printed in the pages of national magazines. It was my job to be the runner of these ad mock-ups to certain offices for approval.

Some of those ads were for some new canned food or meat product that Armour was introducing, or "rolling out," to the public. Being prior to the era of television commercials, much thought was given to the wording, design, and timing of these ads. Back then, magazine ads were seen as an essential method of introducing Armour's new products to America's shoppers.

Companies know the significance of informing the public of a new product. How much more essential it is to announce to the entire human audience the coming of the incarnate Son of God, Jesus of Nazareth! Using the Bible's own words, this study traces the centuries-long "rollout" process of the coming of Jesus Christ, the promised Messiah.

1

FIRST PROMISE

The word "messiah" (with a lowercase m) refers to a person who is regarded as, or who professes to be, a savior or a liberator. The word comes from the Hebrew and is found four times (*Daniel 9:25–26; John 1:41; 4:25*) in some versions of the Bible.

Our entire human enterprise began with the Creator's initiative.

> *In the beginning, God created the heavens and the earth. ... And God said, "Let us make man in our image, after our likeness," ... So God created man in his own image, in the image of God he created him, male and female he created them. ... And God saw everything that he had made, and behold, it was very good. And there was evening and there was morning, the sixth day. (Genesis 1 passim)*

And, for a place to reside,

> *the Lord God planted a garden in Eden ... And out of the ground the Lord God made to spring up every tree that is pleasant to the sight, and good for food. The tree of life was in the midst of the garden, and the tree of the knowledge of good and evil. ... You may*

*surely eat of every tree of the garden, but of the tree
of the knowledge of good and evil, you shall not eat
of it, for in the day that you eat of it you shall surely
die. (Genesis 2 passim)*

But into this "*very good*," idyllic situation, there came a disruption
in God's plan for those persons whom he had formed in his
likeness. There, in that garden, an opponent challenged the
Creator's instruction to the man and woman.

*Now the serpent was more crafty than any other beast
of the field that the Lord God had made. He said to
the woman, "Did God actually say, 'You shall not eat
of any tree in the garden'?" ... So when the woman
saw that the tree was good for food, and that it was a
delight to the eyes, and that the tree was to be desired
to make one wise, she took of its fruit and ate, and
she also gave some to her husband who was with her,
and he ate. (Genesis 3:1,6)*

Because of the serpent's deception, and the man's and woman's
disobedience, God, the Creator, responded by pronouncing and
predicting that this serpent-antagonist would ultimately be fatally
bruised and defeated by the male offspring of the woman he had
deceived.

*The Lord God said to the serpent, "Because you
have done this, cursed are you above all livestock
and above all beasts of the field; on your belly you
shall go, and dust you shall eat all the days of your
life. I will put enmity between you and the woman,
and between your offspring and her offspring; he
shall bruise your head, and you shall bruise his heel."
(Genesis 3:14–15)*

Thus, the scene is set. Because of the enmity and ensuing conflict between these two "*offspring*," an ultimately victorious "*he*" is predicted and promised. *He* would be born of a woman, and would fatally "*bruise the serpent's head*," while the serpent would "*bruise the offspring's heel*." This promised victor, a liberating messiah—**the Messiah**—would bring redress and redemption to God's human family.

Now, with this promise, come the questions:

WHO? — WHERE? — WHEN? — HOW?

2

LENGTHY
ANTICIPATION

God, the Creator, now determined that the conflict between these two offspring, and their lineage, would be resolved in the human arena. The only clue given about the identity of the promised Messiah was that he will be a human, born of a woman.

This suggested that God would begin with the rollout of some human person, but who and where? Conceivably, could God have begun anywhere to choose that special person? Could he have chosen some person of the Nordic race, of the Asian race, or one of some indigenous race? The earliest of written human history, along with archeological evidence, indicates that there was significant human activity, as well as a travel concourse, within the Fertile Crescent, that region stretching from the Nile valley to the twin rivers of Mesopotamia. Perhaps (but certainly not necessarily) that may have focused the Creator's choice?

For whatever reason, God chose a nomadic man of the Semitic race, living in Ur, of Chaldea (in Mesopotamia), by the name of Abram (later to be called Abraham). In his choice, God spoke to him.

*Now the Lord said to Abram, "Go from your country
and your kindred and your father's house to the land
that I will show you. And I will make of you a great
nation, and I will bless you and make your name
great, **so that you will be a blessing**. I will bless
those who bless you, and him who dishonors you I
will curse, and **in you all the families of the earth
shall be blessed**." (Genesis 12:1–3, emphasis added,
see also 22:17–18)*

Thus began what came to be known as the Jewish nation, Israel.
Through special revelations, Abram was given a location and he
began a worshipful relationship with God.

*Then the Lord appeared to Abram and said, "To your
offspring I will give this [Canaan] land." So he built
there an altar to the Lord, who had appeared to him.
(Genesis 12:7)*

From that historic beginning, the Jewish faith and national saga
began to take shape. The patriarchs of Abraham, Isaac, and Jacob
led the family growth, which eventually developed into twelve
distinct families, or tribes. Over the centuries, the whole nation
migrated—first, south into Egypt and eventual slavery. Then, after
an exodus, they journeyed throughout the Sinai Peninsula. Later,
and proceeding north, they crossed over the Jordan River into
Palestinian Canaan, their promised homeland.

All through these migrations, God provided leadership with
Joseph, Moses, and Joshua. During their Sinai journeying, God
revealed himself in varying ways. From Moses' encounter with
God on Mount Sinai, came absolute commandments for worship
and morality. Also, Moses was led to set forth the Passover
observance, and a pattern of worship, with a sacred tabernacle

and consecrated priests. The blood of animal sacrifices was to be offered as atonement for man's garden disobedience and their resulting sinfulness.

Through it all, God was fostering an exclusive, covenant relationship between himself and the emerging nation of Israel. From those earliest days, Israel was divinely destined to become the chosen matrix from which the promised Messiah would emerge and be rolled out to the world.

3

PROPHETIC PREDICTIONS

History and the Old Testament scriptures record that Israel, as a nation, was influenced by their polytheistic, neighboring peoples who worshipped idols. Israel, under some kings, accommodated and even practiced, pagan idolatry. In this, they disobeyed God's commandments and invited his judgments.

God called Israel to righteousness by inspiring prophets to confront them for their disobedience and corruption. Along with predicting harsh judgments, these prophets also confirmed God's covenant love for Israel, and pointed them to the coming Messiah who would eventually *"bruise the serpent's head."* One day, this promised Messiah would be rolled out to Israel.

Isaiah: *"Therefore the Lord himself will give you a sign. Behold, the virgin shall conceive and bear a son, and shall call his name Immanuel." (Isaiah 7:14)*

For to us a child is born, to us a son is given; and the government shall be upon his shoulder, and his name shall be called Wonderful Counselor, Mighty God, Everlasting Father, Prince of Peace. Of the increase of his government and of peace there will be no end, ... (Isaiah 9:6–7)

Jeremiah: "Behold, the days are coming, declares the Lord, when I will raise up for David a righteous Branch, and he shall reign as king and deal wisely, and shall execute justice and righteousness in the land." (Jeremiah 23:5)

Daniel: "Know therefore and understand that from the going out of the word to restore and build Jerusalem to the coming of an anointed one, a prince, there shall be seven weeks. ..." (Daniel 9:25)

Hosea: When Israel was a child, I loved him, and out of Egypt I called my son. (Hosea 11:1)

Micah: But you, O Bethlehem Ephrathah, who are too little to be among the clans of Judah, from you shall come forth for me one who is to be ruler in Israel, whose coming forth is from of old, from ancient days. (Micah 5:2)

Zechariah: Rejoice greatly, O daughter of Zion! Shout aloud, O daughter of Jerusalem! Behold, your king is coming to you; righteous and having salvation is he, humble and mounted on a donkey, on a colt, the foal of a donkey.

Then I said to them, "If it seems good to you, give me my wages; but if not, keep them." And they weighed out as my wages thirty pieces of silver. (Zechariah 9:9; 11:12)

Malachi: "Behold, I send my messenger, and he will prepare the way before me. And the Lord whom you seek will suddenly come to his temple; and the messenger of the covenant in whom

you delight, behold, he is coming, says the Lord of hosts."
(Malachi 3:1)

To balance these prophetic voices, it must be noted that although the Messiah would come as the promised deliverer, it was also predicted that the serpent would *"bruise the heel"* of the woman's offspring.

Note how poignantly Isaiah describes Christ's sufferings in his classic chapter 53:

> ... *a man of sorrows and acquainted with grief ... despised ... rejected ... stricken ... afflicted ... wounded ... crushed ... oppressed ... a lamb led to the slaughter ... numbered with the transgressors.*

As the centuries passed, the nation of Israel vacillated between periods of flourishing and floundering, depending on who was their king. After shameful idolatry and compromise of their exclusive calling, there would often be repentance and reform. That cycle was tragically repeated throughout their history, with a disheartening effect on Israel's moral psyche.

Many of the psalms give voice to Israel's lament and a cry for some deliverer, some savior—the Messiah. One can sense Israel's despair and yearning for help, as written, and prayed:

> *O Lord my God, in you do I take refuge; save me from all my pursuers and deliver me, lest like a lion they tear my soul apart, rending it in pieces, with none to deliver. (Psalm 7:1–2)*

> *My times are in your hand; rescue me from the hand*
> *of my enemies and from my persecutors! Make your*
> *face shine on your servant; save me in your steadfast*
> *love! (Psalm 31:15–16)*

Eventually, after repeated disobedience, rebuke, judgment, reform, and infidelity, God allowed Judah (Israel's southern kingdom) to be besieged and defeated by the Babylonian army in 586 BC. As a result, much of their population was taken to Babylon for a 70-year captivity, or exile. Likely, many in Judah were wondering and praying "If we ever needed this long-promised deliverer, this Messiah, the time is now."

4

PEOPLE TYPES

In his gospel, John profoundly and simply stated that the Messiah would be coming to his own people.

> He came to his own, and his own people did not receive him. (John 1:11)

But, in this earthly setting, who are his own people, and what kind of challenges do they present to the Messiah's rollout? Following are descriptions of some of "his own people":

Scribes: After their 70-year exile, and many years of internal conflict, it appears that many hearts and heads in Israel finally got the message. In time past, Israel had lived fast and loose with God's laws, both displeasing God and jeopardizing their security as a nation. So, they doubled down on a strict adherence to the ceremonial laws written in the Torah (Genesis to Deuteronomy). The scribes were the scholars and teachers who were experts in the specifics of the ceremonial laws.

Pharisees: Through years of political scuffles between the Jews and their secular opponents, the Pharisees were a group who stood for orthodoxy to Judaism's tenets. They became the "monitors" of the ceremonial laws against any deviations. To them, adherence to the letter of the law took precedence over its spirit. They were vigorous critics of the Sadducees and presented a strong, conservative voice throughout Israel.

Sadducees: The Sadducees were the high priests, descendants of an elite, priestly family line, with political connections to the Roman authorities. Any Levite man could become a priest, but never a high priest without this family heritage. Influenced by Greek philosophy, the Sadducees did not believe in angels, nor in the resurrection of the body.

Priests: Being only Levite men, the priests functioned in a ministry in the Jerusalem temple, and in its many instituted practices. In addition, under Roman occupation, they were regarded (with King Herod) as the highest ruling authorities over the nation, somewhat like heads of state.

Publicans: Instead of Rome sending officials to collect its tribute tax, certain of Israel's countrymen were empowered for that task. They were Rome's "IRS agents," and were generally despised as corrupt collaborators in Rome's oppression. Being a publican often required associations with men regarded as "sinners" (see *Luke 5:30*).

Romans: Although not a part of *"his own people,"* they were the decades-long, Gentile, occupying force, with a governing procurator and a military. It is significant that Rome's imprint was evident, both at Jesus' birth, and at his crucifixion!

Jesus of Nazareth, the promised Messiah, coming with no human credentials, was to encounter these groupings of people, and became increasingly popular among the rank and file inhabitants of Israel. Some in these groups were the self-proclaimed guardians of Israel's traditions, and strongly opposed Jesus' teachings about *"fulfillment"* of ceremonial laws (see *Matthew 5:17*). These groups, together with the common crowd, and the Roman presence, made up the milieu into which the Messiah was to be rolled out.

So, as the centuries passed, throughout Israel's struggles, along with all of humanity's yearning for a savior, there was a divine agenda for the rollout of the promised Messiah.

> *But when the fullness of time had come, God sent forth his Son, born of woman, born under the law, to redeem those who were under the law, so that we might receive adoption as sons.* (Galatians 4:4–5)

$$\boxed{5}$$

BIRTH TIME

God's Messiah was to be the offspring of some woman. And now, in the time for him to be rolled out, who should be the birth mother? Might she be expected to be, say, the daughter of some prominent priestly family in Jerusalem? Such a birth by her would certainly be heralded by the Jewish people as a glorious, national development. His birth would become a most welcome vindication of Israel's struggles and might even be the means for the nation Israel to overthrow Rome's oppressive rule.

Instead, though, God had his own design. The rollout of the Messiah began in the village of Nazareth in Galilee. It was there that angel Gabriel visited a devout, young maiden, named Mary. The angel's message to her was:

> "Greetings, O favored one, the Lord is with you! ....
> Do not be afraid, Mary, for you have found favor
> with God. ... And behold, you will conceive in your
> womb, and bear a son, and you shall call his name
> Jesus. He will be great and will be called the son of
> the Most High. And the Lord God will give to him
> the throne of his father David. And he will reign over
> the house of Jacob forever, and of his kingdom there
> will be no end." (Luke 1:28–33, passim)

ODE TO NAZARETH

O quiet village of Nazareth, obscure
beside a Rome, an Athens,
or even a Jerusalem,
Men could know and visit you, yet they pass by
On their way to their appointments of importance.

Yet ... in your dark streets one night,
Came that angelic visitor to a humble
maiden of tender years,
Chosen was she from among all the ages,
And from among all the daughters of Israel.
With her, God set an intimate and ultimate appointment,
And, by a quiet, gentle touch, was begun
The loftiest design ever, begun with
God before time began.

There and then, O Nazareth, did you become a pivot,
Upon which all history turned.
In you, a small obedience brought
forth a torrent of glory,
For from you was God's gift given—
Jesus the Nazarene.

(by James Blaine)

By the angel's words, Mary was awestruck in knowing that she was to give birth to a son who was to have a divine destiny. He was to be called the "*Son of the Most* High," which she knew to be "Messiah time." In her touching "Magnificat" (*Luke 1:46–55*), Mary pondered the meaning of her pregnancy for herself, but more importantly, for its significance for all of Israel. At its close, Mary said of God's design:

> "He has helped his servant Israel, in remembrance of his mercy, as he spoke to our fathers, to **Abraham and to his offspring** forever." (Luke 1:54–55, emphasis added)

As her pregnancy progressed, Joseph, her betrothed husband-to-be, being a just man and much devoted to Mary, was quite perplexed by this personal development. Providentially, an angel appeared to him in a dream in order to calm his fears, and to bring him up to speed on this mysterious and most sacred situation.

> But as he considered these things, behold, an angel of the Lord appeared to him in a dream, saying, "Joseph, son of David, do not fear to take Mary as your wife, for that which is conceived in her is from the Holy Spirit. She will bear a son, and you shall call his name Jesus, for he will save his people from their sins." (Matthew 1:20–21)

Because of developments in Rome's jurisdiction over its outlying provinces, it became necessary for Joseph, being of King David's lineage, to travel and register in Bethlehem. That was miles away from his home, but so prophetically significant. Mary, being in the later trimesters of her pregnancy, and to avoid any local criticism, accompanied Joseph on his journey. Her time for giving birth there came in much less-than-favorable earthly circumstances. But, in glorious fulfillment, Mary delivered there her tiny newborn—the long-promised Messiah—the eternal Son of God now veiled in human flesh—and among us.

Announcing the birth of any child is a cause for much joy. But, announcing the birth, the rollout, of the promised Messiah was to be truly very special. This historic news was not given to scribes and priests in Jerusalem, but to some shepherds near Bethlehem, men without high status or privilege. An angel suddenly appeared to them one night to say:

> ... *"Fear not, for behold, I bring you good news of great joy that will be for all the people. For unto you is born this day in the city of David a Savior, who is Christ the Lord. And this will be a sign for you: you will find a baby wrapped in swaddling cloths and lying in a manger." And suddenly there was with the angel a multitude of the heavenly host praising God and saying, "Glory to God in the highest, and on earth peace among those with whom he is pleased!" (Luke 2:10–14)*

After their overpowering, angelic visitation, with its special rollout announcement, the shepherds resolved to go into Bethlehem.

> *And they went with haste and found Mary and Joseph, and the baby lying in a manger. And when they saw it, they made known the saying that had been told them concerning this child. And all who heard it wondered at what the shepherds told them. ... And the shepherds returned, glorifying and praising God for all they had heard and seen, as it had been told them. (Luke 2:16–18, 20)*

Also, there was another sign of his birth—an astronomical sign in the appearance of a new or brighter star. To some eastern learned men, likely Gentiles, that star indicated the birth of the *"king of the Jews"* (Matthew 2:1–3). That motivated them to travel to

Jerusalem, the Jewish capital, to acknowledge and worship him. After being directed to Bethlehem, that star finally led them to the baby's location. With exuberant delight, they finally found Mary and her baby. Falling down in worship before him, they opened their treasures: gold, frankincense and myrrh. By their travel and worship, these men were a significant witness and response to the rollout of the long-promised Messiah.

Then, that old garden serpent, in the guise of King Herod, conspired to bruise the Messiah's head, and thwart his rollout. But, with angelic protection and guidance, Joseph and Mary fled to Egypt, escaping Herod's cruel carnage of all of Bethlehem's infant boys (see *Matthew 2:1–18*).

6

THE QUIET YEARS

Between the return to Nazareth from Egypt and Jesus' public ministry, the scriptures record very little about the Messiah during that period. It simply states:

> And Jesus increased in wisdom and in stature and in favor with God and man. (Luke 2:52)

At age twelve, Jesus and his parents came to Jerusalem for the annual Passover feast. After searching three days for Jesus among the crowds, Joseph and Mary finally found him in the temple, in conversation with some scribes:

> ... sitting among the teachers, listening to them and asking them questions. And all who heard him were amazed at his understanding and his answers. (Luke 2:46–47)

Picture these respected scribes, advanced in age, status, and learning, having serious exchanges with a precocious, twelve-year-old boy from (backwater?) Nazareth! Is there any doubt that one topic of their conversations was the Messiah's coming? And what irony, then, that their promised Messiah was already being rolled out, and was sitting right there among them!

Consider now these **assumptions** about Jesus during his three-decade life in Nazareth:

- Jesus lived as part of Joseph and Mary's family, along with his siblings.

- Jesus would be seen and acknowledged as Joseph's son.

- Jesus likely participated in activities of village life, along with others, both young and old.

- Jesus attended the local synagogue and had access to scrolls of written scripture.

- Jesus quite likely had some involvement in Joseph's carpentry work and would perform some manual tasks.

- In all personal interactions with others, Jesus would be kind, discreet, truthful, and wise.

- As a child, as an adolescent, and as an adult, Jesus became acclimated to life as a human.

Based on these assumptions, as Jesus experienced normal village life of that time and place, he became fully immersed in life as a human being. Even being the Son of God incarnate, he would likely be seen by his village peers, as just a serious, but normal, young adult male—in clothing, in appearance, and in demeanor. He truly was the Son of Man, as well as the Son of God.

At about age thirty, Jesus left Nazareth and journeyed eastward to the spot on the Jordan River where John was baptizing.

7

ADVANCE MAN

For rolling out some new product in the marketplace, there will be some advance initiative or advertisement. The same is true for the Messiah's rollout. It was John the Baptist who was to "*prepare the way of the Lord*" (Matthew 3:3).

> There was a man sent from God, whose name was John. He came as a witness, to bear witness about the light, that all might believe through him. (John 1:6–7)

John was born of devout parents with an angelic involvement. As an adult, he began a preaching ministry that could be likened, somewhat, to a "charismatic revival." His ministry was radically different and caught the attention of common folk, as well as "temple headquarters" in Jerusalem. John's preaching locale was the wilderness, where he lived a spartan lifestyle.

Crowds came out to hear John preach, "*Repent, for the kingdom of heaven is at hand*" (Matthew 3:2). Included in his audience were: priests, Levites, soldiers, publicans, and even Sadducees and Pharisees, as well as any who may have become jaded by the prescribed requirements for the "hand washings" (see Matthew 15:2) and "sabbath keepings" (see Luke 6:1–2) of the ceremonial laws. John's message was "good news," and any who repented were baptized in the Jordan River. They would then turn to *"love the Lord God with all their heart, soul, mind and strength,"* and to *"love their neighbor"* in practical and compassionate ways, as their self (see *Mark 12:30–31*).

John's ministry heightened the prospect of a coming Messiah as Israel's hope. Some of John's converts wondered, and even asked him, *"Are you the Christ"*? (i.e., the Messiah?). John quickly and clearly answered:

> ... *"I am not the Christ."* ... *"I baptize you with water, but he who is mightier than I is coming, the strap of whose sandals I am not worthy to untie. He will baptize you with the Holy Spirit and fire."* (*John 1:20, Luke 3:16*)

> Then *Jesus came from Galilee to the Jordan to John, to be baptized by him.* ... *The next day he saw Jesus coming toward him, and said, "Behold, the Lamb of God, who takes away the sin of the world!"* (*Matthew 3:13, John 1:29*)

8

HERE AT LAST

At age 30, Jesus was poised to begin the public part of his rollout. After being baptized by a human prophet, he then received divine endowment and recognition.

> *And when Jesus was baptized, immediately he went up from the water, and behold, the heavens were opened to him, and he saw the Spirit of God descending like a dove and coming to rest on him; and behold, a voice from heaven said, "This is my beloved Son, with whom I am well pleased." (Matthew 3:16–17)*

Often, new commercial products, as a part of their rollout, are put through a period of testing. Having been baptized and divinely anointed, Messiah Jesus was then led by the Spirit into the wilderness to be tempted by the devil for 40 days, all with angelic oversight.

Then, that old garden serpent, whom we now know as the devil, confronted Jesus with attractive proposals:

"If you are the Son of God ..."

The devil first tempted Jesus to **experience pleasure** by using his divine ability to change stones into edible loaves of bread. Jesus responded with a scriptural quotation:

> It is written, "Man shall not live by bread alone, but by every word that comes from the mouth of God."

The devil then tempted Jesus to **flaunt his position** as God's Son by jumping off a high temple pinnacle and expect the angels to catch him.

To this "stunt," Jesus answered:

> Again, it is written, "You shall not put the Lord your God to the test."

The devil finally tempted Jesus to **acquire possessions** of all the kingdoms of the world.

> "All these I will give you, if you will fall down and worship me."

Jesus replied to this proposal:

> "For it is written, 'You shall worship the Lord your God and him only shall you serve.'" (Luke 4:1–10, passim)

The devil proposed to derail and deter the Messiah's rollout, but Jesus used scripture to oppose that strategy.

Jesus returned to Nazareth and to his home synagogue, where he revealed himself as other than just Joseph's son. There, he read from a scroll of Isaiah:

> *"The Spirit of the Lord is upon me, because he has anointed me to proclaim good news to the poor. He has sent me to proclaim liberty to the captives and recovering of sight to the blind, to set at liberty those who are oppressed, to proclaim the year of the Lord's favor."*

With all eyes upon him, Jesus returned the scroll, and said:

> *"Today this Scripture has been fulfilled in your hearing." (Isaiah 61:1–2; Luke 4:18–19, 21)*

By this public reading, he revealed his full identity to his earthly hometown (and to all people), and continued his rollout to a wider world.

As he began his public ministry, Jesus needed no fanfare or introduction because John the Baptist was his announcer. Neither did he need any **endorsement** by the temple authorities because he had received a heavenly **endowment** and the Spirit's **empowerment.**

Jesus issued the same clarion call which John the Baptist preached to all who would hear:

> *From that time Jesus began to preach, saying, "Repent, for the kingdom of heaven is at hand." (Matthew 4:17)*

Early on, after a night of prayer, Jesus was led to call some men to be his disciples, beginning with some fishermen on Galilee's north shore:

> *… he called his disciples and chose from them twelve, whom he named apostles: Simon, whom he named Peter, and Andrew his brother, and James and John, and*

> Philip, and Bartholomew, and Matthew, and Thomas,
> and James the son of Alphaeus, and Simon who was
> called the Zealot, and Judas the son of James, and Judas
> Iscariot, who became a traitor. (Luke 6:13–16)

Andrew was the first disciple to sense Jesus' real identity:

> He [Andrew] first found his own brother Simon and
> said to him, "We have found the Messiah" (which
> means Christ). (John 1:41)

Jesus began the next part of his rollout with a tour of teaching
situations—in small groups, in synagogues, and sometimes to a
multitude. Often, he used familiar parable stories to teach about
the "kingdom of God." As a prelude to his seminal Sermon on the
Mount (Matthew 5–7), we read:

> Seeing the crowds, he went up on the mountain, …
> [a]nd he opened his mouth and taught …
>
> And when Jesus finished these sayings, the crowds
> were astonished at his teaching, for he was teaching
> them as one who had authority, and not as their
> scribes. (Matthew 5:1–2; 7:28–29)

In his teaching among his Jewish audiences, Jesus made one point
very clear.

> "Do not think that I have come to abolish the Law or
> the Prophets; I have not come to abolish them but to
> fulfill them." (Matthew 5:17)

Now, in addition to his teaching, Jesus began to "speak" by
performing miraculous acts, specifically by supernaturally healing

some personal afflictions, or by altering certain physical conditions. In John's Gospel, Jesus' miracles are called "signs," and are a significant evidence of his personal rollout (see John 4:48; 20:30).

In Jesus' many miracles, he:

- Changed water into vintage wine at a wedding. (*John 2:1–11*)

- Delivered a man possessed by demons. (*Luke 4:33–36*)

- Gave sight to a man born blind. (*John 9:1–7*)

- Healed a leper of his disease. (*Mark 1:40–44*)

- Fed a multitude from a boy's lunch, and with leftovers. (*Matthew 14:13–21*)

- Calmed a storm on the Sea of Galilee. (*Matthew 8:23–27*)

- Healed a paralytic at Bethesda's pool. (*John 5:1–9*)

- Raised a deceased daughter back to life. (*Matthew 9:18–26*)

> *And he went throughout all Galilee, **teaching** in their synagogues and **proclaiming** the gospel of the kingdom and **healing** every disease and every affliction among the people. So his fame spread throughout all Syria, and they brought him all the sick, those afflicted with various diseases and pains, those oppressed by demons, those having seizures, and paralytics, and he healed them. And great crowds followed him from Galilee and the Decapolis, and from Jerusalem and Judea, and from beyond the Jordan. (Matthew 4:23–25, emphasis added)*

9

FALLOUT FROM
THE ROLLOUT

Newton's Law—to every action, there will be an equal and opposite reaction—thus goes this long-understood law. To something as significant as the Messiah's rollout in Israel, one would expect that there would be a pronounced reaction. Indeed, the resulting fallout was a fourfold reaction.

Early in his teaching tours, with crowds growing in Israel, a multitude came to Galilee's shore to hear Jesus teach. With so many pressing in, he spoke to them from a boat to deliver this parable:

> "Listen! Behold, a sower went out to sow. And as he sowed, some seed fell along the path, and the birds came and devoured it. Other seed fell on rocky ground, where it did not have much soil, and immediately it sprang up, since it had no depth of soil. And when the sun rose, it was scorched, and since it had no root, it withered away. Other seed fell among thorns, and the thorns grew up and choked it, and it yielded no grain. And other seeds fell into good soil and produced grain, growing up and increasing and yielding thirtyfold and

*sixtyfold and a hundredfold." (Mark 4:3–8, see also
Matthew 13:18–23; Luke 8:5–15)*

It seems clear that Jesus spoke this parable to provide an understanding of the various responses to him and his teaching. And now, in generations to come, any person who receives the "gospel seed," may identify themselves in one of these four soils:

> *And he said to them, "Do you not understand this parable? … The sower sows the word. And these are the ones along the path, where the word is sown: when they hear, Satan immediately comes and takes away the word that is sown in them. And these are the ones sown on rocky ground: the ones who, when they hear the word, immediately receive it with joy. And they have no root in themselves, but endure for a while; then, when tribulation or persecution arises on account of the word, immediately they fall away. And others are the ones sown among thorns. They are those who hear the word, but the cares of the world and the deceitfulness of riches and the desires for other things enter in and choke the word, and it proves unfruitful. But those that were sown on the good soil are the ones who hear the word and accept it and bear fruit, thirtyfold and sixtyfold and a hundredfold." (Mark 4:13–20)*

Hard-packed pathway soil

Seed must penetrate the soil in order to grow. Some human "soil" is resistant to the germination of gospel seeds because of rigid, long-held beliefs or prejudices. Also, one's track record of living style may be so established that it would injure the ego to allow the good seed to be received.

Jesus also warned that the garden serpent devil is an active opponent who will work to prevent any germination of the seed, leading to a fruitfulness that would glorify the Creator.

Shallow and rocky soil

Some seeds germinate and grow rapidly, but when their needy roots search deeper for nourishment, they encounter only a layer of rock and wither down.

Reports of Jesus' miracles and teaching spread like wildfire throughout Israel. Crowds followed him, and many had first-hand knowledge of his miracles. His teachings, even though a challenge to the temple establishment, had popular support. But, with such strong official opposition, many were deterred and lost enthusiasm for the Messiah.

Crowded and weedy soil

Some seeds get off to a good start, germinating and growing. But soon, there is competition for space and food. The supermarket of life offers an abundance of opportunities, pleasures, and things to choose from. Noxious weeds are ever present and the "better" crowds out the "best." And all this competition simply stifles any growth of the gospel seed.

A wealthy, young man once came to Jesus, asking what he should do in order to inherit eternal life. Jesus replied to him:

> ... "You lack one thing: go, sell all that you have and give to the poor, and you will have treasure in heaven;

and come, follow me." *Disheartened by the saying,*
he went away sorrowful, for he had great possessions.
(Mark 10:21–22)

Receptive and productive soil

The focus for this soil is, not only to be seed-friendly, but to look expectantly to the harvest which promises to be abundant in varying degrees. In Jesus' other teachings, there is a harvest-like result to being receptive to the gospel seed:

> "... *whoever believes in him should not perish but have **eternal life**.*" *(John 3:16, emphasis added)*

> *Come to me, all who labor and are heavy laden, and I will give you **rest**. Take my yoke upon you, and learn from me, ... and you will find **rest for your souls**. (Matthew 11: 28–29, emphasis added)*

Like the seed in the pathway soil, Jesus' ministry was met with stubborn resistance. It came consistently from those in the temple establishment, and from their Pharisee supporters. Because they could not deny the reality of Jesus' miracles, nor his growing popular support, they found some basis for opposing him. To them, Jesus defied the ceremonial law's specific commandments, and so, he was criticized for:

- Healing a paralytic man (and others) on the Sabbath. (John 5:1–9)

- Eating with publicans and "sinners." (Matthew 9:10–13)

- Plucking heads of grain to eat on the Sabbath. (*Luke 6:1–5*)

- Allowing a "sinful" woman to anoint his feet. (*Luke 7:39*)

- Not washing hands before eating. (*Matthew 15:1–2*)

- Teaching his gospel in the temple courtyard. (*Matthew 21:23*)

They even stooped to accuse Jesus of exorcizing demons from a man by the power of Beelzebub.

> *The Jews said to him, "Now we know that you have a demon! Abraham died, as did the prophets, yet you say, 'If anyone keeps my word, he will never taste death.' Are you greater than our father Abraham, who died? And the prophets died! Who do you make yourself out to be?" ... Your father Abraham rejoiced that he would see my day. He saw it and was glad." So the Jews said to him, "You are not yet fifty years old, and have you seen Abraham?" Jesus said to them, "Truly, truly, I say to you, before Abraham was, I am." (John 8:52–53, 56–58)*

As Jesus taught and ministered, and as his popularity soared, he knew that being the woman's offspring, he was destined for some ultimate bruising:

> *"Now is my soul troubled. And what shall I say? 'Father, save me from this hour'? But for this purpose I have come to this hour. Father, glorify your name." ... (John 12:27–28)*

And at a later time, while going to Jericho, with a similar concern:

And taking the twelve, he [Jesus] said to them, "See, we are going up to Jerusalem, and everything that is written about the Son of Man by the prophets will be accomplished. For he will be delivered over to the Gentiles and will be mocked and shamefully treated and spit upon. And after flogging him, they will kill him, and on the third day he will rise." (Luke 18:31–33)

For about three years, Jesus' rollout ministry continued with much popular support. On his final visit to Jerusalem, Jesus directed his disciples to arrange a procession into the city with him riding a young colt. How fitting that the chorus being sung, or chanted, by the multitude in that procession was **"Hosanna"** (see John 12:13). That Hebrew word meaning, *"save now"* was an expression of tribute, but it was also a heart cry for the Messiah. It was based on *Psalm 118:26*:

Blessed is he who comes in the name of the Lord! We bless you from the house of the Lord.

Many in that throng knew Jesus as a gifted teacher and a worker of miracles, but some probably had no inkling that they were participating in the rollout of the long-promised Messiah.

Later in that week, as the Passover time drew near, Jesus planned to share the occasion as a last meal with his followers:

And when the hour came, he reclined at table, and the apostles with him. And he said to them, "I have earnestly desired to eat this Passover with you before I suffer. For I tell you I will not eat it until it is fulfilled in the kingdom of God." And he took a cup, and when he had given thanks he said, "Take this, and divide it among yourselves. For I tell you that from now on I will not drink of the fruit of the vine until the kingdom of God comes." And he took bread, and when he had given thanks, he broke it and gave it to them, saying, "This is my body, which is given for you. Do this in remembrance of me." And likewise the cup after they had eaten, saying, "This cup that is poured out for you is the new covenant in my blood." (Luke 22:14–20)

Jesus' growing popularity, along with his claims of deity, eventually became intolerable to his adversaries. So, in response, a devilish plot formed among the temple's highest authorities:

Now the Feast of Unleavened Bread drew near, which is called the Passover. And the chief priests and the scribes were seeking how to put him to death, for they feared the people. Then Satan entered into Judas called Iscariot, who was of the number of the twelve. He went away and conferred with the chief priests and officers how he might betray him to them. (Luke 22:1–4)

Later, in another garden (Gethsemane), Jesus came with some disciples to pray.

Then he said to them, "My soul is very sorrowful, even to death; remain here, and watch with me." And going a little farther he fell on his face and prayed, saying, "My Father, if it be possible, let this cup pass from me; nevertheless, not as I will, but as you will." ... he went away and prayed for the [second and] third time, saying the same words again. Then he came to the disciples and said to them, "Sleep and

> *take your rest later on. See, the hour is at hand, and*
> *the Son of Man is betrayed into the hands of sinners.*
> *Rise, let us be going; see, my betrayer is at hand."*
> *(Matthew 26:38–39, 44–46)*

After Jesus' arrest in the garden, he was brought before the high priests, elders, Herod, and finally to Governor Pilate. The reports of Jesus' teaching about "*the kingdom of God*" had reached even into the palace.

> *Now Jesus stood before the governor, and the governor*
> *asked him, "Are you the King of the Jews?"*

To this, Jesus replied:

> *"Do you say this of your own accord, or did others*
> *say it to you about me?" … "My kingdom is not of*
> *this world." … "For this purpose I was born, and*
> *have come into the world … to bear witness to the*
> *truth."*
>
> *… he [Pilate] went back outside to the Jews, and told*
> *them, "I find no guilt in him." (Matthew 27:11; John*
> *19:33–38, passim)*

Following this contrived trial, the garden serpent enemy dealt Messiah Jesus a final, cruel bruise, intending it to be fatal and conclusive.

> *So they took Jesus, and he went out, bearing his own*
> *cross, to the place called The Place of a Skull, which*
> *in Aramaic is called Golgotha. There they crucified*
> *him, and with him two others, one on either side, and*
> *Jesus between them. Pilate also wrote an inscription*

and put it on the cross. It read, "Jesus of Nazareth, the King of the Jews." (John 19:16–19)

For three mournful days following Jesus' crucifixion, the hearts of his followers were heavy, and their hopes were dashed. But the Messiah's rollout was about to take another turn. The next morning, some women proposed to come with spices to wrap his body. But they found Jesus' tomb empty, and there, two men, dazzlingly dressed, announced to them:

> ... "Why do you seek the living among the dead? He is not here, but has risen. ..." (Luke 24:5–6)

Then, the risen Messiah, with his rollout complete:

> ... that he was raised on the third day in accordance with the Scriptures, and that he **appeared** to Cephas, then to the twelve. Then he **appeared** to more than five hundred brothers at one time, most of whom are still alive, though some have fallen asleep. Then he **appeared** to James, then to all the apostles. Last of all, as to one untimely born, he **appeared** also to me [the apostle Paul]. (1 Corinthians 15:4–8, emphasis added)

Finally, with his disciples and other believers:

> And he led them out as far as Bethany, and lifting up his hands he blessed them. While he blessed them, he parted from them and was carried up into heaven. And they worshiped him and returned to Jerusalem with great joy, and were continually in the temple blessing God. (Luke 24:50–53)

*The true light, which gives light to everyone, was coming into the world. He was in the world, and the world was made through him, yet the world did not know him. He came to his own, and his own people did not receive him. But to **all who did receive him, who believed in his name**, he gave the right to become children of God, who were born, not of blood nor of the will of the flesh nor of the will of man, but of God.*

And the Word [Messiah] became flesh and dwelt among us, and we have seen his glory, glory as of the only Son from the Father, full of grace and truth. (John 1:9–14, emphasis added)

And now, for those who believe in and receive the risen Messiah:

*… Christ Jesus is the one who died—more than that, who was raised—who is at the right hand of God, who indeed is **interceding for us**. (Romans 8:34, emphasis added)*

*Consequently, he is able to save to the uttermost those who draw near to God through him, since he always lives to **make intercession for them**. (Hebrews 7:25, emphasis added)*

Now, all believers await Jesus' victorious **dénouement.**

*For the grace of God **has appeared** [rolled out?], bringing salvation for all people, training us to renounce ungodliness and worldly passions, and to live self-controlled, upright, and godly lives in the present age, **waiting for our blessed hope, the appearing***

of the glory of our great God and Savior Jesus Christ, who gave himself for us to redeem us from all lawlessness and to purify for himself a people for his own possession who are zealous for good works. (Titus 2:11–14, emphasis added)

CONCLUSIONS

The prophecy for a coming Messiah was not written in one clear, conclusive statement, but was, rather, a composite one. It came together piecemeal over centuries. This is well stated in the opening lines of the Hebrews epistle: …

> Long ago, at many times and in many ways, God spoke to our fathers by the prophets, but in these last days he has spoken to us by his Son, whom he appointed the heir of all things, … (Hebrews 1:1–2)

So, with the prophetic specifics, the Jews apparently modeled the coming Messiah to be in full compliance with the ceremonial laws and its practices. In other words, Israel was expecting—a true "Jewish" Messiah, in total alignment with their laws. Instead, Jesus came as the **whole world's Messiah**, opening the doorway to God's kingdom.

> For God did not send his Son into the world to condemn the world, but in order that the world might be saved through him. (John 3:17)

Such a misjudgment has resulted in the Jewish rejection of Jesus.

When one views the Israel of Jesus' day objectively, some factors come into clear view. First, there is the lingering, national memory of being besieged and defeated by a Gentile force. That was followed by the humiliation of being transported as captives to a foreign land. Now, being occupied by Roman rule and troops was a further threat to their sovereignty and established religion. A defensive posture was to be maintained at all costs.

As John the Baptist's challenging message became known, it was preparatory, and somewhat isolated—in the wilderness. But, as Jesus of Nazareth began his teaching tour, north and south, it was embraced by growing crowds, and authenticated by obvious miracles. He taught that the ceremonial law was to be kept in the heart, and not by its specifics. Efforts to repudiate or silence him were fruitless. Even though being the promised Messiah, he was perceived as a growing threat to Israel's national honor, traditions, and beliefs.

In the Jewish stance of being a chosen people, with Abraham as their father, the Jewish people may have overlooked or reinterpreted two little words: **"so that"**.

Going back to the original call to Abraham in Genesis, God clearly stated that there was a clear **destiny** in the formation of their new nation:

> "And I will make of you a great nation, and I will bless you and make your name great, **so that** you will be a blessing. ... and in you all the families of the earth shall be blessed." (Genesis 12:2–3, emphasis added)

So now, these centuries later, how shall/should Israel determine its God-given purpose in becoming, and being, a distinctive voice for the Creator God, and for his love for peoples and nations.

I would offer this thoughtful response to this question:

Israel's ultimate destiny in becoming a distinctive people was, and is: First, **so that** they should live out as a covenant people, exalting the one true and living God to all nations, and second, **so that** they would become the chosen matrix for the birth and life of Jesus Christ, the **world's Messiah**. And now, in reflection on history, how truly blessed have been/are *"all the families of the earth"* hearing and knowing of **their** Messiah!

The conflict between the Creator and the garden serpent devil was destined to be marked by some ultimate bruising. The devil plotted to finally and fatally bruise God's offspring (Jesus) at Calvary. But what actually occurred at Calvary, though, in indescribable agony, was the final and fatal bruise to the serpent's head. It was there that the spotless Lamb of God became the atoning sacrifice for the sins of all people, and thereby, finally defeated the devil's power by Jesus' death and resurrection:

> *The last enemy to be destroyed is death.*
> *(1 Corinthians 15:26)*

> *"Χαρισ τω θεω επι τη ανεκδιηγητω αυτου δωρεα!"*
> *"Thanks be to God for his inexpressible gift!"*
> *(2 Corinthians 9:15)*

ACKNOWLEDGMENTS

Dr. Robert G. Willhoft and Mrs. Faith B. Willhoft, my son-in-law and daughter, provided encouragement and personal care throughout. I am especially indebted for their valuable, and special assistance, both literary and technical.

ABOUT THE AUTHOR

Rev. James Blaine is a retired, ordained minister in the Wesleyan Church. He has served as pastor in Wesleyan and United Methodist churches, both in the United States and in Canada. He is a graduate of Marion College (now Indiana Wesleyan University) and Asbury Theological Seminary. He earned an advanced degree at Western Theological Seminary (MI) in Biblical Literature.

With his training and experience, in this writing, he offers his observations and conclusions concerning the timing and manner of Jesus' coming as the promised Jewish Messiah, and its significance for everyone today.

TO THE READER

This study originated in trying to better understand the reason for the opposition by the various Jewish authorities, in that first century, to the person and ministry of Jesus Christ, their promised Messiah, as noted in John 1:11 *"He came to his own, and his own people did not receive him."*

Printed in the United States
by Baker & Taylor Publisher Services